Sport Climbing

John Nichols

Steadwell Books

Raintree Steck-Vaughn Publishers

A Harcourt Company

Austin · New York

www.raintreesteckvaughn.com

Published by Raintree Steck-Vaughn Publishers,
an imprint of Steck-Vaughn Company.

Library of Congress Cataloging-in-Publication Data
Nichols, John, 1966-
     Sport climbing/John Nichols.
          p. cm.-- (Extreme sports)
     Includes bibliographical references (p.) and index.
     ISBN 0-7398-4691-4
     1. Rock climbing--Juvenile literature [1. Rock climbing.] I. Title. II.
Extreme sports (Austin, Tex.)

GV200.2 N53 2001
796.52'23--dc21   2001019818

Printed and bound in the United States of America
1 2 3 4 5 6 7 8 9 10 WZ 05 04 03 02 01

Produced by Compass Books

Photo Acknowledgments
Tony Donaldson:10, 20, 26, 28, 30, 32, 34, 36, 38, 40, 42 bottom, 43 top, 43 bottom; Corey Rich: title page, 12, 14, 16; SD Tourism/Chad Coppess: 20; Corbis: 4, 12-13, 27, 42 top.

Content Consultant
Simon Fryer
Program Manager, American Mountain Guides Association

Contents

Routes and Gyms

Outdoor routes can either be natural rock or special walls made by people. Most sport climbers like to climb outdoors on natural rock. Indoor routes are usually found in special places called climbing gyms.

Indoor climbing gyms began to appear in many large cities during the mid-1980s. They made it possible for climbers to work on many different routes. They could do this in one place, no matter what the weather

was like outside, and at different times of the day. Today, there are climbing gyms all over the world. The invention of climbing walls and gyms has made it easier for people to try sport climbing.

How Sport Climbing Began

In the 18th century, rock climbers trained on small outdoor routes to gain strength and to sharpen their skills in order to climb large mountains. These short climbs were like sport climbing, but sport climbing was not yet considered a sport of its own.

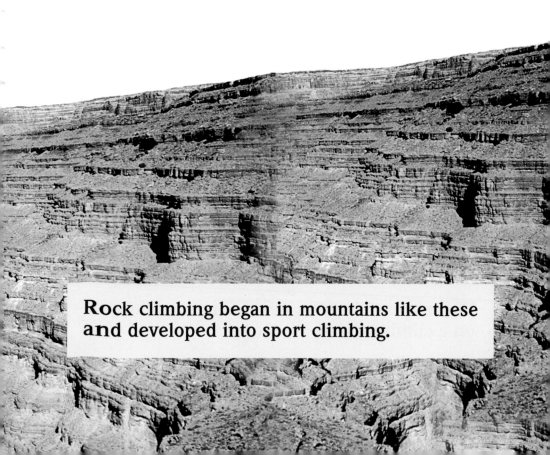

Rock climbing began in mountains like these and developed into sport climbing.

Sport climbers need to be smart in order to think their way out of difficult spots.

Who Can Become A Sport Climber?

Good climbers work hard to build strong, flexible bodies. Flexible means they can bend and stretch easily.

Sport climbers eat healthy foods. They stay flexible by stretching every day. They build strength by using other forms of exercise, such as pull-ups, sit-ups, and push-ups.

Climbers need to build endurance. Endurance is the ability to work hard for a long period of time. Climbers build it by working on difficulty and speed routes several times a week. Running and swimming also help build endurance.

It is important that climbers rest during their training. Their bodies need time off in order to grow stronger. Rest allows a body to recover, giving it the ability to grow even stronger.

Climbers need to practice in different ways
to learn how to control their bodies

Skills To Learn

Experienced and new climbers use their bodies differently. Beginners mainly use their arms. Experienced climbers mainly use their legs. Leg muscles are bigger and stronger than arm muscles. Climbers who use their legs more often do not get tired as quickly.

Experienced climbers learn to control their bodies. They make sure they do not reach too far in any direction. This could cause them to lose their balance.

Sport climbers use many different skills to go up a route. Even the smallest of bumps on a wall can help a good climber get to the top the fastest.

Good climbers learn how to "flag." This is done by sticking a leg out in one or another direction. Climbers hold the leg out to improve their balance.

Good climbers learn how to switch their feet and hands. This is done by taking the foot or hand farthest away from the next hold and putting it closest to the next hold. This foot or hand is then used to reach for the hold. This helps climbers reach farther.

"Edging" is another skill good climbers learn. To do this, they use the inside or outside edges of their shoes to get a grip on the small pieces of rock or wall. Then they push themselves up.

Where Do I Train?

Sport climbers of all skill levels need places to train. In the United States, there are 17 training centers approved by a group called the American Sport Climbing Federation (ASCF). There are also hundreds of private schools where climbers can learn and practice.

One of the reasons sport climbing is popular is because it can be done all over the world. There is natural rock that can be climbed in all 50 states. Climbers see some of the most beautiful places in the world. This helps make every new climb exciting. There are 28 countries that have indoor climbing gyms.

Sometimes sport climbers will repel down natural rock they have climbed or set up a route on.

Professional sport climbers need to be flexible to reach handholds and footholds.

Who Are the Professional Sport Climbers?

Some **professional** sport climbers earn their living by climbing. A professional is someone who makes money doing something others do for fun. Professionals usually enter several major competitions each year. It takes them many weeks to get into top shape. They plan out their training. They want to be in the best shape for the most important competitions.

Pro climbers do not make millions of dollars like some other professional sports stars. They often need other jobs to earn a living. Only the very best pro sport climbers are able to earn a living from their sport.

Pros compete at many different levels. They have to win at local events before they can enter national ones. Those who do well in national events may be chosen for their country's team. Then they go to **World Cup** events.

> These sport climbers are climbing at the X Games.

World Championships

Every two years, a World Championship is held. Men's and women's champions for each kind of sport climbing—difficulty and speed—are crowned there.

Most of the top sport climbers in the world are from Europe. Sport climbing there is as popular as football is in the United States.

What Does it Take?

Most professionals train for several hours a day at least four or five times a week. The best climbers are usually between 20 and 35 years old. Most of them have been pros for five years or more.

Jason and Tiffany Campbell are two of the best sport climbers in the United States. They are married and train together and also teach climbing. Jason began climbing at age 11. Tiffany did not start until her mid-20s.

Tiffany believes that beginning climbers should not give up. "Do not waste time being embarrassed or shy," she says. "Everyone starts out a beginner, and it can be frustrating. Just give yourself a chance to get better and improve."

Climber Profile: Vladamir Zakharov

Vladimir Zakharov was ranked first in the world in men's speed climbing in 2000. He was third in the same year in the UIAA World Cup rankings. He was born in 1972 in the Ukraine. He began climbing at age 15. In 2000, he placed third in the UIAA World Cup competition. In 1999, he placed first in the UIAA World Championship.

Sport climbers sometimes have to pause to think about how they will proceed.

Getting Better

Jason began his climbing career as a traditional, or trad, climber. These climbers go up longer routes and use heavier equipment. Today, Jason says he is trying to become a champion sport climber. "If you look at how long other countries have been involved, and how far they have come, it makes me think that in a few years we [climbers in the United States] will be doing some incredible things," he says.

Pro Climbing

To climb an indoor wall, pros must make sure of several things. It is important to choose a route that is difficult but not impossible. It is also important to think through what skills will be needed to climb the route. On indoor walls, pros will use their hands and feet in many ways to move steadily up the route

One kind of climb is called an **on-site climb**. This means the pro has not seen the route before climbing it. The pro only has a little time to plan the climb.

On an indoor wall, pros are usually able to clearly see the handholds and footholds. This makes planning the climb easier.

Even when stuck, professional sport climbers know that their equipment will not let them fall very far.

Rest and Crux Areas

On any route, some parts are harder or easier than others. The easiest parts are called rest areas. This is where pros can stop and take time to think about their next move. The more difficult areas are called **crux** areas. Pros need to use both their bodies and minds at these tougher parts.

Climbing Outdoors

Climbing an outdoor route is hard in other ways. In an on-site outdoor climb, pros must think about weather conditions, such as wind, rain, or heat. These can all make the climb more difficult.

Pros always think before they move. If they move when they do not need to, they waste energy.

Many people think that pro climbers never fall. This is not true. In fact, the best climbers often will fall. Safety ropes and the belayer keep them safe.

Did You Know?

Did you know that more and more young people are becoming sport climbers? In 1996, there were close to 50 Junior Competitions held in the United States. How do we know that the number of young climbers is rising? In 1999, there were over 300 Junior Competitions.

One of the reasons sport climbing has become popular is because millions of people have seen it on television at the X Games.

Competing in Sport Climbing

The group that runs sport climbing around the world is called the International Union of Alpinist Associations (UIAA). An alpinist is a person who likes to climb hills or mountains. The UIAA runs the World Cup and World Championships and ranks climbers. It is made up of people from over 60 countries. It controls competitions for all other kinds of climbing, too.

In the United States, sport climbing is controlled by the American Sport Climbing Federation (ASCF). It runs climbing events for people of all skill levels. It holds local, regional, and national events to find champions.

The ASCF competitions help to choose climbers for the U.S. Climbing Team. The top eight men and women are invited to join it. They represent the United States at World Cup events.

Judges pay close attention to climbers like this one to see how they choose to handle a route.

Judging a Climb

Sport climbers are judged on both their speed and their ability to climb difficult routes. In some competitions, the fastest climber wins. In others, the winner is the one who makes it to the top in the best way. Speed climbers are usually judged only on time. Climbers on difficulty routes are usually judged by how high they get and how well they make their way up.

One problem with judging is that different countries use different ratings for routes. This makes it difficult to compare climbers from different countries.

Climber Profile: Chris Bloch

Chris Bloch is the top speed climber in the United States. He has not yet been ranked among the world's top 40 speed climbers. He was born in 1971 in Stockton, California. He began climbing at the age of 13. In 1999, he placed first in the Summer X Games.

39

▲ Experienced climbers learn special ways of keeping their balance while reaching for the next hold.

Competitions And Prizes

Sport climbing grew in popularity after being seen on television as part of the X Games. The X Games are extreme sports competitions held every year that are shown and **sponsored** by the sports television network ESPN. The X Games are not an official ASCF or UIAA event. Even so, they have brought millions of new fans to the sport.

Such attention has brought more prize and sponsor money into sport climbing. A sponsor is a company that pays a sport climber to use or advertise what it sells.

Becoming Popular

In the early 1980s, sport climbing was still done mainly as a way to train for traditional climbing. It is now one of the fastest growing sports in the world. More people join the UIAA and the ASCF every year. Sport climbers hope that sport climbing will become an Olympic sport one day.

Climber Profile: Elena Ovchinnikova

Elena Ovchinnikova is the top senior women's difficulty route climber in the United States. Senior climbers are older climbers. In 2000, she was ranked seventh in the world. She was born in 1965 in Russia. She began climbing at the age of 22.

Quick Facts About
Sport Climbing

There are over 1 million climbers in the United States today. About one-third of them are women.

There are about 1,000 places where people can climb indoors in the United States.

The ASCF helps run over 50 competitions each year in the United States.

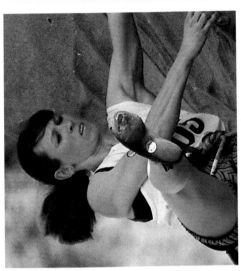

Over 30 countries hold national championships in sport climbing.

California has more than 50 indoor climbing gyms. This is the most of any state in the United States.

Internet Sites and Addresses

American Sport Climbing Federation
http://www.mindspring.com/~ascf

Archive of Rock Climbing Moves And Tips
http://chvc2.netfirms.com/climb.htm

EXPN
http://expn.go.com/

Indoor Rock Climbing
http://www.rockworks.co.uk/p04/indoor-rock-climbing.html

International Council for Competition Climbing
http://www.icc-info.org/

Sport Climbing Basics
http://www.rei.com/reihtml/LEARN_SHARE/climb/clsportop.html?stat=7505

The American Alpine Club
710 Tenth Street, Suite 100
Golden, CO 80401

American Safe Climbing Association
P.O. Box 7421
Mammoth Lakes, CA 93546

American Sport Climbing Federation
710 Tenth Street, Suite 130
Golden, CO 80401

Junior Competition Climbing Association
P.O. Box 19145
Portland, OR 97280-0145

Books to Read

Ashton, Steve. *Climbing*. All Action, Minneapolis: Lerner, 1992. This book describes the history, techniques, equipment, and excitement of rock, sport, ice, and mountain climbing.

Brimner, Larry Dane. *Rock Climbing*. Danbury, CT: Franklin Watts, 1997. This book presents a brief description of rock climbing as a sport that requires little equipment, appeals to all ages, and is considered to be mentally as well as physically challenging.

Index